There are two
ways of spreading light:
to be the candle or
the mirror that reflects it.

Edith Wharton (1862–1937)
American writer

9   8   7
Digit on the right indicates the number of this printing.

ISBN 1-56138-700-2

Illustrations by Valerie Spain
Designed by Susan E. Van Horn
Edited by Tara Ann McFadden
Printed in the United States

This book may be ordered by mail from the publisher.
Please add $2.50 for postage and handling.
But try your bookstore first!

Running Press Book Publishers
125 South Twenty-second Street
Philadelphia, Pennsylvania 19103-4399

Reflections

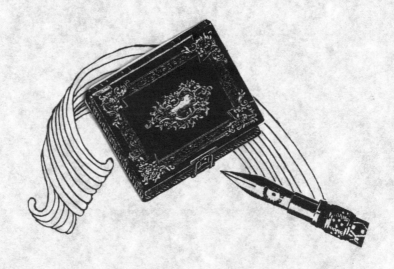

A Woman's Own Journal, with Illustrations and Quotes

RUNNING PRESS
PHILADELPHIA · LONDON

I was not looking for my dreams to interpret my life, but rather for my life to interpret my dreams.

Susan Sontag (b. 1933)
American writer

. . . it isn't until you come to a spiritual understanding of who you are —
not necessarily a religious feeling, but deep down the spirit within —
that you can begin to take control.

Oprah Winfrey (b. 1954)
American talk show host

Trust in yourself. Your perceptions
are often far more accurate than
you are willing to believe.

Claudia Black
20th-century American writer

There is not one big cosmic meaning for all,

there is only the meaning we each give to our life. . . .

To give as much meaning to one's life as

possible is right to me.

Anaïs Nin (1903–1977)
French-born American writer

$\mathcal{L}$ife is so constructed, that the event does not, cannot, will not, match the expectation.

Charlotte Brontë (1816–1855)
English writer

I have learned to live each day as it comes,

and not to borrow trouble by dreading tomorrow.

It is the dark menace of the future that makes cowards of us.

Dorothy Dix (1861–1951)
American writer

People are their own people. They've got their own personalities, and if you try to put strings on them, you run that person away.

You've got to give; you've got to trust; there must be respect.

Tina Turner (b. 1940)
American singer and songwriter

Trouble is a sieve through which we sift our acquaintances. Those too big to pass through are our friends.

Arlene Francis (b. 1908)
American actress

. . . friendships aren't perfect and yet they are very precious.

For me, not expecting perfection all in one place was a great release.

Letty Cottin Pogrebin (b. 1939)
American writer

You can't go around
hoping that most people have
sterling moral characters.
The most you can hope
for is that people will
pretend that they do.

Fran Lebowitz (b. 1951)
American writer

W_e

want

people

to

feel

with

us

more

than

to

act

for

us.

George Eliot [Mary Ann Evans] (1819–1880)
English writer

One's life has value so long as one attributes value to the life of others, by means of love, friendship, indignation, and compassion.

Simone de Beauvoir (1908–1986)
French writer

The story of a love is not important—what is important is that one is capable of love.

It is perhaps the only glimpse we are permitted of eternity.

Helen Hayes (1900–1993)
American actress

$\mathcal{W}$hen you love someone all your saved-up wishes start coming out.

Elizabeth Bowen (1899–1973)
Irish writer

*In every relationship,
there are times when a little honesty
is better than a lot.*

Marilyn vos Savant (b. 1946)
American writer

There is more difference within the sexes than between them.

Ivy Compton-Burnett (1892–1969)
English writer

$\mathcal{I}$f it is your time love will track

you down like a cruise missile.

Lynda Barry
20th-century American cartoonist

You fall in love with someone, and part of what you love about him are the differences between you; and then you get married and the differences start to drive you crazy.

Nora Ephron (b. 1941)
American writer

No partner in a love relationship . . . should feel that he has to give up an essential part of himself to make it viable.

May Sarton (1912–1995)
Belgian-born American writer

For a certain type of woman who risks losing her identity in a man, there are all those questions . . . until you get to the point and know that you really are living a love story.

Anouk Aimee (b. 1932)
French actress

A woman has got to love a bad man once or twice in her life, to be thankful for a good one.

Marjorie Kinnan Rawlings (1896–1953)
American writer

$\mathcal{A}$ woman

without a man

is like a fish

without a bicycle.

Gloria Steinem (b. 1934)
American writer and editor

$\mathcal{I}$ don't need an overpowering,

powerful, rich man to feel secure.

I'd much rather have a man

who is there for me,

who really loves me,

who is growing,

who is real.

Bianca Jagger (b. 1945)
Nicaraguan-born American actress

I think anybody bright would realize that you've got to be charming and wonderful and fun and adorable and pleasant and terrific—some of the time.

Helen Gurley Brown (b. 1922)
American writer and editor

Charm is often despised but I can never see why. No one has it who isn't capable

of genuinely liking others, at least at the actual moment of meeting and speaking.

Charm is always genuine; it may be superficial but it isn't false.

P. D. James (b. 1920)
English writer

The especial genius of women
I believe to be electrical in movement,
intuitive in function, spiritual in tendency.

Margaret Fuller (1810–1850)
American journalist

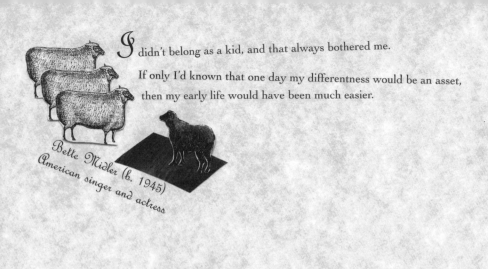

I didn't belong as a kid, and that always bothered me.

If only I'd known that one day my differentness would be an asset,
then my early life would have been much easier.

Bette Midler (b. 1945)
American singer and actress

To have one's individuality completely ignored
is like being pushed quite out of life.
Like being blown out as one blows out a light.

Evelyn Scott (1893–1963)
American writer

... how many different climates of feeling one can go through in one day.

Anne Morrow Lindbergh (b. 1906)
American writer

When one door of happiness closes another opens; but often we look so long at the closed door that we do not see the one which has been opened for us.

Helen Keller (1880–1968)
American writer and lecturer

I don't think that . . . one gets a flash of happiness once, and never again; it is there within you. . . .

Isak Dinesen [Karen Blixen] (1885–1962)
Danish writer

In search of my
lost innocence,
I walked out a door.
At the time I believed
I was looking for a purpose,
but I found instead
the meaning of choice.

Liv Ullman (b. 1938)
Swedish-born American actress

Never go back to a place

where you have been happy.

Until you do it remains alive for you.

Agatha Christie (1891–1975)
English writer

Happiness is not a matter of events; it depends on the tides of the mind.

Alice Meynell (1847–1922)
English poet

Happiness is an insecure thing and yet we don't reject it, we allow it to overwhelm us, to confuse. . . .

Carole Morin (b. 1964)
Scottish writer

Joy seems to me a step beyond happiness—happiness is a sort

of atmosphere you can live in sometimes when you're lucky.

Joy is a light that fills you with hope and faith and love.

Adela Rogers St. Johns (1894–1988)
American writer

The more the years go by,
the less I know.
But if you give explanations
and understand everything,
then nothing can happen.
What helps me go forward
is that when I stay receptive,
I feel that anything can happen.

Anouk Aimee (b. 1932)
French actress

Besides learning to see, there is another art to be learned—not to see what is not.

Maria Mitchell (1818–1889)
American astronomer

In the effort to give good
and comforting answers
to the young questioners
whom we love, we very
often arrive at good
and comforting answers
for ourselves.

Ruth Goode (b. 1905)
American writer

The only interesting answers are those which destroy the questions.

Susan Sontag (b. 1933)
American writer

Show me a person who has never
made a mistake and I'll show you someone
who has never achieved much.

Joan Collins (b. 1933)
English-born American actress

The way I see it, if you want the rainbow, you gotta put up with the rain.

Dolly Parton (b. 1946)
American singer and actress

. . . if you ask, you also must be able to live with the answers.

Patricia D. Cornwell (b. 1956)
American writer

. . . no point in picking the apple if you don't want to see how it tastes.

Toni Morrison (b. 1931)
American writer

I think it's very important

to be positive about

everything in your life

that's negative.

Barbra Streisand (b. 1942)
American singer, actress, and film director

. . . that is what learning is.

You suddenly understand something

you've understood all your life,

but in a new way.

Doris Lessing (b. 1919)
English writer

If life is to be enjoyed . . . then later isn't really an option.

Julie Kurnitz
20th-century American actress

Who knows whether there will be a better time? The time is always now.

Erica Jong (b. 1942)
American writer

*I*f only we could all accept that there is no difference between us where human values are concerned.

Whatever sex. Whatever the life we have chosen to live.

Liv Ullman (b. 1938)
Swedish-born American actress

*I*t is very easy to forgive others their mistakes;

it takes more grit and gumption to forgive

them for having witnessed your own.

Jessamyn West (b. 1907)
American writer

Regret is an appalling waste of energy; you can't build on it; it's only good for wallowing in.

Katherine Mansfield (1888–1923)
New Zealand-born English writer

It's never too late to apologize.

Joy Fielding (b. 1945)
American writer

You make choices, you have regrets, the very least you can do is know what they are. . . . Otherwise, what's the point?

Abby Frucht (b. 1957)
American writer

*I*f you haven't failed, you haven't tried very hard.

Shirley Hufstedler (b. 1925)
American judge

*I*t isn't the big pleasures that count the most,

it's making a big deal out of the little ones.

Jean Webster (1876–1916)
American writer

You have to . . . learn the rules of the game. And then you have to play it better than anyone else.

Dianne Feinstein (b. 1933)
United States Senator

$\mathcal{L}$ife is a game to see how far you can get

on the board before the opponent catches you.

That is the fun—matching wits but

really liking each other.

Joan Rivers (b. 1933)
American comedienne and writer

One can never speak enough of the virtues, the dangers, the power of shared laughter.

Françoise Sagan (b. 1935)
French writer

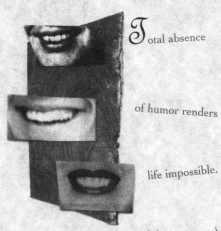

$\mathcal{T}$otal absence

of humor renders

life impossible.

Colette [Sidonie-Gabrielle] (1873–1954)
French writer

Those who do not know how to weep with their whole heart don't know how to laugh either.

Golda Meir (1898–1978)
Israeli prime minister

Great loves too must be endured.

Coco Chanel (1883–1970)
French designer

"I think patience is what love is," he said, "because how could you love somebody without it?"

Jane Howard (b. 1935)
American writer

Instead of getting hard
ourselves and trying to compete,
women should try and give their
best qualities to men—bring them
softness, teach them how to cry.

Joan Baez (b. 1941)
American singer and songwriter

One of my theories is that men love with their eyes; women love with their ears.

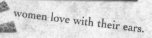

Zsa Zsa Gabor (b. 1923)
Hungarian-born American actress

The mark of a true crush . . . is that you fall in

love first and grope for reasons afterward.

Shana Alexander (b. 1925)
American writer

It is a risky business loving someone a lot. There may be only one thing more dangerous: not loving at all.

Joyce Maynard
20th-century American writer

The trouble is all in the knob at the top of our bodies.

Margaret Atwood (b. 1939)
Canadian writer

$\mathcal{R}$elationship is a pervading and changing mystery . . . brutal or lovely, the mystery waits for people wherever they go, whatever extreme they run to.

Eudora Welty (b. 1909)
American writer

When she stopped conforming
to the conventional picture of femininity
she finally began to enjoy being a woman.

Betty Friedan (b. 1921)
American writer

No one should have to dance backward all their lives.

Jill Ruckelshaus (b. 1937)
American lawyer

𝒜 woman is like a teabag. You don't know her strength until she is in hot water.

Nancy Reagan (b. 1923)
First Lady of the United States

$\mathcal{T}$rue

strength

is

delicate.

Louise Nevelson (1900–1988)
American sculptor

Once, power was considered a masculine attribute. In fact, power has no sex.

Katherine Graham (b. 1917)
American publisher

If I have to, I can do anything.

Helen Reddy (b. 1941)
Australian-born American singer

$\mathcal{I}$don't think of myself as a poor

deprived ghetto girl who made good.

I think of myself as somebody who

from an early age knew I was responsible

for myself, and I had to make good.

Oprah Winfrey (b. 1954)
American talk show host

It had long since come to my attention that people of

accomplishment rarely sat back and let things happen to them.

They went out and happened to things.

Elinor Smith (b. 1908)
American aviator

I have never understood why "hard work" is supposed to be pitiable. . . .

You get tired, of course, often in despair, but the struggle, the challenge,

the feeling of being extended as you never thought you could be,

is fulfilling and deeply, deeply satisfying.

Rumer Godden (1907–1998)
English writer

. . . the final forming of a person's character lies in their own hands.

Anne Frank (1929–1945)
German diarist

When one is a stranger to oneself then one is estranged from others too.

Anne Morrow Lindbergh (b. 1906)
American writer and aviator

*I*f you do not tell the truth about yourself  you cannot tell it about other people.

Virginia Woolf (1882–1941)
English writer

I wish that every human life might be pure transparent freedom.

Simone de Beauvoir (1908–1986)
French writer

The way we were treated as small children is the way we treat ourselves the rest of our life.

Alice Miller
20th-century American writer

I have no romantic feelings about age.
Either you are interesting at any age or you are not.
There is nothing particularly interesting about
being old—or being young, for that matter.

Katharine Hepburn (b. 1909)
American actress

Some memories are realities, and are better than anything that can ever happen to one again.

Willa Cather (1873–1947)
American writer

Do not deprive me of my age. I have earned it.

May Sarton (1912–1995)
Belgian-born American writer

If you give up you're never going to get there. . . . no one ever succeeds who gave up.

Judith Henry Wall (b. 1940)
American writer

The excursion is the same when you

go looking for your sorrow as when

you go looking for your joy.

Eudora Welty (b. 1909)
American writer

Peace is not won by those who fiercely guard

their differences but by those who with open

minds and hearts seek out connections.

Katherine Paterson
20th-century American writer

. . . there is not enough darkness in the world to snuff out the light of even one small candle.

Marian Wright Edelman (b. 1939)
American writer

Reflections

A Woman's Own Journal, with Illustrations and Quotes